ALL ABOUT PENGUINS

To every child who loves penguins, or is just curious about them.

And to Sanccob, the first penguin chick I ever raised.

You were the first penguin I loved, but far from the last.

————————

-DD

All About
Penguins

Discover Life on Land and in the Sea

Dyan deNapoli

Illustrations by Ray Shuell

R
ROCKRIDGE
PRESS

Do you know what kind of animal a penguin is? Penguins are birds, but they cannot fly. Like all birds, penguins' **ancestors** were dinosaurs. About 160 million years ago, some dinosaurs began to **evolve** and change into birds that could fly. Then about 60 million years ago, some of those birds became penguins. Penguins have been on Earth for a VERY long time!

Have you ever met a penguin? This is a King penguin. This large penguin lives on South Georgia Island in the southern Atlantic Ocean. South Georgia Island is very beautiful. It is also very cold, windy, and **remote**, so no people live there. King penguins are just one of 19 kinds, or **species**, of penguins on Earth.

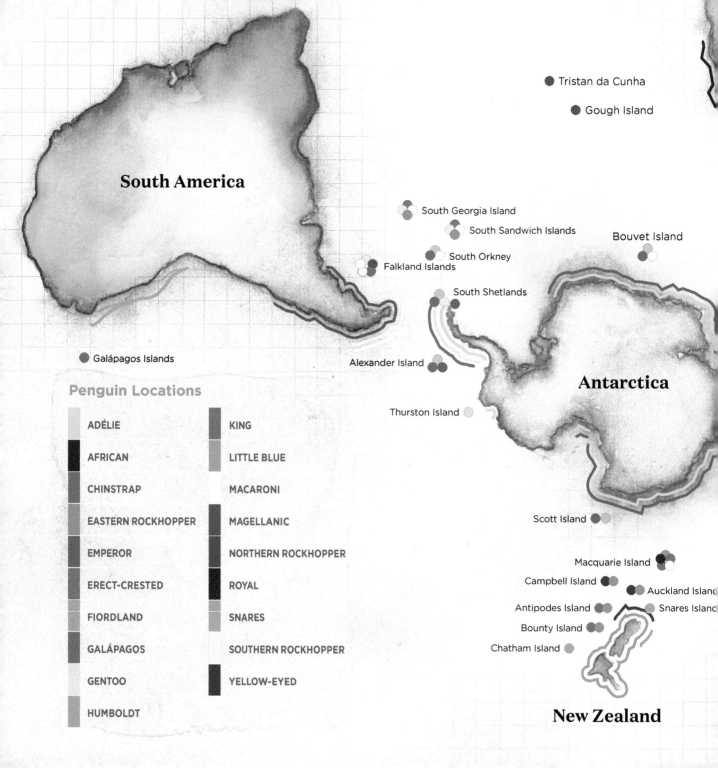

South America

Tristan da Cunha

Gough Island

Bouvet Island

South Georgia Island

South Sandwich Islands

South Orkney

Falkland Islands

South Shetlands

Alexander Island

Antarctica

Thurston Island

Galápagos Islands

Penguin Locations

ADÉLIE	KING
AFRICAN	LITTLE BLUE
CHINSTRAP	MACARONI
EASTERN ROCKHOPPER	MAGELLANIC
EMPEROR	NORTHERN ROCKHOPPER
ERECT-CRESTED	ROYAL
FIORDLAND	SNARES
GALÁPAGOS	SOUTHERN ROCKHOPPER
GENTOO	YELLOW-EYED
HUMBOLDT	

Scott Island

Macquarie Island

Campbell Island

Auckland Island

Antipodes Island

Snares Island

Bounty Island

Chatham Island

New Zealand

Africa

Madagascar

Marion Island

Prince Edward Island

Crozet Islands

Kerguelen Islands

Amsterdam Island

Heard Island

Saint Paul Island

Tasmania

Australia

All penguins live in the southern hemisphere. An imaginary line, called the **equator**, divides the Earth into two halves. Each half is called a **hemisphere**. Everything above the equator is the northern hemisphere, and everything below the equator is the southern hemisphere.

Penguins live in all sorts of climates in all sorts of places. They live in South America, South Africa, Australia, New Zealand, Antarctica, and on many islands in the southern oceans. Galápagos penguins live right along the equator on the Galápagos Islands, where it is very hot! A few Galápagos penguins build their nests JUST above the equator. They are the only penguins that ever enter the northern hemisphere.

Did You Know? Most scientists used to think there were 17 penguin species. But they now believe there are 19! New tests showed there are actually three different species of Rockhopper penguins.

Have you ever seen a penguin? Penguins look a lot alike. They all have white bellies, and most of them have black backs. So, how can you tell them apart?

Penguins come in many different sizes, and each species has its own special markings. This means their feathers have slightly different patterns and colors, especially on their heads and necks. You only need to see a penguin's head to be able to tell what species it is!

The largest penguin is the Emperor. They are almost 4 feet tall. Emperor penguins have orange and yellow feathers on their cheeks and necks, and their beaks are black and pink. The smallest penguin is the Little Blue. They are less than a foot tall. Sometimes they are called Fairy penguins.

Did You Know? Even though penguins have webbed feet, they *never* paddle them like a duck. Instead, penguins point their webbed feet down one at a time to change direction.

Have you ever seen a penguin swim? Penguins are designed for swimming in the ocean. Their bodies are shaped like footballs. Their short, stiff wings slice through the water like blades. Penguins' **webbed feet** are at the bottom of their bodies. When they are swimming, their feet stick out straight behind them. They move their feet when they want to steer or change direction.

Sometimes penguins swim by leaping in and out of the water like dolphins. This is called porpoising. Just like dolphins and porpoises, penguins can't breathe underwater. Every time they leap out of the water, they take a breath.

Penguins spend most of their lives at sea. They hunt in the ocean, and even rest on the surface of the water. Most penguins only come onto land once a year, when it is time to raise their babies and to **molt**. Molting is when birds shed their feathers and grow in new ones.

Even though penguins can't fly, they are still birds. We know this because they have feathers. Birds are the ONLY animals with feathers. Like all birds, penguins also lay eggs, and have beaks and wings.

Birds that fly have hollow bones. This makes them light enough to fly. Penguins have solid bones. This helps penguins dive deep in the ocean, but it makes them too heavy to fly. Their short wings are also much too small to ever lift them off the ground. But when they flap them up and down to swim, they look like they are flying through the water!

Have you ever seen a penguin dive? They may not be able to fly, but they are expert swimmers and divers. Penguins can swim faster and dive deeper than any other bird! Most penguins can dive down to about 300 feet—the height of the Statue of Liberty—and hold their breath for up to three minutes.

Did You Know? Penguins have salt glands under the skin above their eyes. These special glands remove extra salt from their bodies. This means penguins can drink as much salty ocean water as they want!

Emperor penguins are true seabird champions! They can dive 1,800 feet deep—almost the height of two Eiffel towers—and can hold their breath for up to 30 minutes!

Have you ever seen a penguin waddle? They are very graceful in the water, but very awkward on land. They stand upright because their legs are at the bottom of their bellies.

Even though you can't see them, penguins have knees! Penguins waddle because they always keep their knees bent like they're squatting. This makes their legs look very short. It also makes them tilt from side to side when they walk. Try it . . . you'll waddle, too!

Penguins can walk long distances. Some walk many miles. Emperor penguins can walk 100 miles! Most penguins can even run in short bursts. Crested penguins often move faster by jumping or bouncing. They look like they have springs!

Penguins in Antarctica sometimes flop down onto their bellies on the snow and ice, and slide by pushing off with their wings and feet. This is called tobogganing. They can move much faster this way.

Did You Know? Emperor penguins huddle together for warmth in the freezing Antarctic. All other penguins (even in Antarctica) like standing farther apart. Penguins that live where it's hot hold out their wings, and pant (like a dog) to cool off.

90 F

King penguins live where it is very cold, but there isn't much snow where they molt and raise their young. Different penguin species live in different **climates** and temperatures. Some live where it is very hot, some live where it is freezing, and some live in climates that are in between.

No matter where they live, all penguins hunt in very cold waters. A thick layer of **blubber** (or fat) under their skin helps keep them warm in the ocean.

Penguins have thousands of small, stiff feathers
that lay over each other like scales on a fish. They
use their beaks to **preen**, or straighten them.
Their feathers have tiny hooks that lock them
together, like Velcro. This stops cold water and
air from reaching their skin.

Have you ever seen a penguin without feathers? Once a year, penguins shed ALL of their feathers and grow in new ones. This takes a few weeks, and is called a **catastrophic molt**. Penguins can't hunt for food during this time, because they don't have feathers to keep them warm in the ocean. They have to eat lots of extra food beforehand. The extra fat keeps them alive while they're molting.

Did You Know? Penguin predators at sea include orcas (or killer whales), seals, and sharks. Penguin predators on land include large birds like skuas, giant petrels, and sheathbills.

Have you ever seen a penguin hide? Penguins have dark backs and white bellies. These colors help them blend into their surroundings and hide from animals hunting them at sea. Animals that hunt other animals are called **predators**.

When a predator swimming above a penguin looks down, the penguin's dark back blends in with the dark ocean below. When a predator swimming below a penguin looks up, the penguin's white belly blends in with the ice or sunlit waters above. This special **camouflage** is called **countershading**.

When penguins come onto land to raise their families and molt, they gather in large groups called **colonies**. Different species gather in colonies of different sizes. Some might have a few dozen penguins. King penguin colonies have thousands and thousands of penguins!

Once penguins start laying eggs, this gathering place is called a **rookery**.

Have you ever *heard* a penguin? Penguins communicate using their bodies *and* their voices. Each species makes its own special call. Little Blues bark and trill. African penguins bray like donkeys. Northern Rockhoppers honk. King penguins trumpet!

Each penguin also has a unique voice. Their voice is different from every other penguin around them. This is how penguins find their families in a huge crowded colony. With so many birds calling to each other, penguin colonies are *very* noisy places!

Did You Know? All penguin parents take turns taking care of their eggs, except for Emperor penguins. The Emperor *dad* holds his mate's egg on his feet all by himself for over two months. He does not eat during that whole time!

Every year, penguins come to land when it is time to start a family. Each male penguin sings a special song to attract a female penguin. After he finds his perfect mate, she lays one or two eggs.

Most penguins lay two eggs in a nest built from pebbles or plants, or dug into the earth. But King and Emperor penguins only lay one egg, which they **incubate** on top of their feet under a pouch of loose skin. Almost all penguin parents take turns keeping their eggs warm and dry for one or two months, depending on what species they are. Then their **chicks** are born.

Have you ever met a baby penguin?
When a penguin chick is ready to
hatch, it taps on the inside of the egg
with its beak. *Tap, tap, tap, tap, tap!*

Penguin chicks have a hard, white tip on their beak called an egg tooth. This helps them break a hole through their shells, which is called **pipping**. It can take a few days for a chick to hatch all the way out of its shell! Their egg tooth falls off a few days later.

Did You Know? Penguin chicks are born covered with soft, fluffy feathers called down. This down is not waterproof, so they cannot go into the ocean. Once their waterproof feathers grow in, they are **juveniles** and must survive on their own. One year later, they become adults.

Penguin parents take turns hunting for food and feeding their chicks by **regurgitating**, or throwing up partly digested seafood into their mouths. After about one month, parents leave their chicks alone to go hunt at sea. The chicks in the colony gather together for safety until their parents return with bellies full of food for them. A group of these chicks is called a **crèche**.

Did You Know? Like all birds, penguins don't have teeth. Instead, penguins have rubbery prongs on their tongues and the roofs of their mouths to help them hold on to slippery seafood!

Have you ever seen a penguin eat? Different penguins eat different foods, depending on where they live. Penguins eat fish, squid, and **krill**.

Krill is a small animal that looks like shrimp. There is a *lot* of krill in the very cold waters around Antarctica, so that is what most Antarctic penguins eat.

Krill

Fish

Squid

Penguins are amazing animals! But most penguin species are **threatened** or **endangered**. This means there are far fewer of those penguins on Earth than there used to be. This is because some human activities harm the places they live. Humans often pollute the air and the oceans. They also take too much fish and krill from the sea, which means penguins have less to eat.

There are many ways humans help penguins, though. Rescue centers save penguins that get caught in oil spills at sea. Volunteers clean up beaches to keep plastic out of the ocean. Scientists studying penguins help us understand these special birds and what we can do to protect them.

You can help penguins and other animals by taking care of the environment where you live!

Penguin Fun Facts

 **Adélie:** This feisty penguin species is named after the wife of the French explorer who discovered it in 1840. Adult Adélie penguins have a thin ring of white feathers around their eyes.

 **African:** The only penguin that lives on the **continent** of Africa. They are sometimes called "beach donkeys" because they nest on beaches and bray like donkeys.

 **Chinstrap:** Named for the thin band of black feathers that runs under its chin. This makes it look like it is wearing a black cap with a strap.

 **Emperor:** The world's largest penguin, and the only penguin that raises its chick during the freezing Antarctic winter!

Erect-crested: This penguin is named for the short, spiky crest feathers that stand straight up on the sides of its head.

Fiordland: This is the only crested penguin with small white stripes of feathers on its cheeks.

Galápagos: This penguin lives in the hottest temperatures along the equator. It is the world's only tropical penguin species!

Gentoo: This penguin has an orange beak and pink feet. It is bold and curious. When people visit their colonies, these penguins waddle right over to greet them.

Humboldt: Like all banded penguins, the Humboldt penguin has a handful of black feathers scattered on its chest and belly. You can tell individual banded penguins apart by their unique pattern of black feathers, which even grow back in the same exact pattern every time they molt!

King: King penguin chicks have brown downy feathers. They look SO different from their parents, that early explorers thought chicks and adults were two different species of penguins!

Little Blue: The world's smallest penguin. It stands just eight inches tall and weighs two to three pounds. And its feathers are actually blue!

Macaroni: In the 1700s, stylish Englishmen wore tall wigs with long curls. These men were called *the Macaroni* (like the pasta). Early English explorers named the Macaroni penguin after these men, because its crest feathers reminded them of the fancy wigs.

 **Magellanic:** Named after the Portuguese explorer Ferdinand Magellan. He had never seen a penguin before, and he didn't know if it was a fish, a bird, or a mammal!

 **Eastern Rockhopper:** Like all Rockhoppers, this penguin gets its name from the way it hops so expertly across rocks. It lives on the islands south of New Zealand, Australia, and South Africa.

 **Northern Rockhopper:** This is the largest of the three Rockhopper species. It has longer crest feathers than the other two, and it lives farther north.

 **Southern Rockhopper:** Like the Eastern Rockhopper, the Southern Rockhopper has short, spiky crest feathers above its eyes. This penguin is found on islands off the tip of South America.

Royal: Some scientists believe the Royal penguin is actually a type of Macaroni penguin. They look the same, except for the color of their faces. The Macaroni penguin has a black face, and the Royal penguin has a white face.

Snares: This crested penguin lives where there are trees with very low branches. They sometimes climb up and rest on the lowest branches near the ground.

Yellow-eyed: This large penguin has yellow feathers on its entire head and face—even its eyes are yellow! It is the only penguin species that does not like to nest near other penguins.

Penguin Life Cycle

Glossary

ancestor: An animal or person that other animals or people have descended from and are related to.

blubber: A thick layer of fat that helps keep an animal warm.

camouflage: Colors, patterns, and/ or shapes that help an animal hide by blending into its surroundings.

catastrophic molt: When a bird loses and replaces all of its feathers at once.

chick: A baby bird. Penguins are chicks until their downy feathers fall out and their waterproof feathers grow in.

climate: Typical patterns of weather in different places on the planet (such as hot and wet, or cold and dry).

colony: A group of penguins (or other animals) that gather together on land.

continent: A large body of land, often surrounded by ocean. There are seven continents on Earth.

countershading: A type of camouflage where an animal has a dark back and a light belly.

crèche: A group of older chicks gathered together for warmth and safety while their parents hunt at sea.

endangered: When very few of a type of animal or plant is left on Earth.

equator: An imaginary line that divides the Earth in half at its widest point.

evolve: To slowly change over time into a different form. Evolution often takes millions of years.

hatch: To break out of an egg. This is how chicks are born.

hemisphere: Half of the Earth. The Earth is divided into the northern and southern hemispheres.

incubate: To keep an egg warm, dry, and protected so the chick inside can grow.

juvenile: A young animal. A penguin chick becomes a juvenile when its first waterproof feathers grow in. It is on its own after that.

krill: A small sea creature that looks like a shrimp.

mate: A partner. When two penguins choose each other to raise chicks together, they have become mates.

molt: To shed and replace feathers, fur, skin, shell, or outer skeleton. Birds molt their feathers.

pipping: The moment a chick breaks a hole through its egg.

predator: An animal that hunts and eats other animals.

preen: To comb through and organize hair, feathers, or fur. Birds use their beaks to preen their feathers.

regurgitate: To throw up partially digested food.

remote: Very far from places where people live.

rookery: A place on land where birds gather to raise their chicks.

species: A group of closely related animals (or plants) that are basically the same as each other.

threatened: Similar to endangered, but not quite as serious. This means there are far less of a threatened animal or plant on Earth than there used to be.

webbed feet: Feet that have connecting skin between the toes (like a fan).

About the Author

Dyan deNapoli (a.k.a. The Penguin Lady) is a penguin expert, TED speaker, and award-winning author. Her book for adults, *The Great Penguin Rescue*, is about her experiences saving 40,000 penguins from an oil spill in South Africa. Dyan took care of the penguins at Boston's New England Aquarium for nine years. She has been teaching about penguins for 25 years, and is a frequent guest on radio, TV, and podcasts internationally. Dyan has been to Antarctica four times, twice as a lecturer for National Geographic. She visited South Georgia Island in 2019, and was pretty excited when some King penguins waddled over and nibbled on her camera! Visit her website at ThePenguinLady.com to learn more about penguins and penguin rescue centers.

About the Artist

Ray Shuell has held a lifelong interest in watercolor painting, holding his first one-man show in 1975 followed by many more mixed and one-man shows.

He was born in the UK and ran his own business before teaching fine art to eager college students. He moved to France in 2007, where he realized a long-held ambition to run his own art school in the beautiful countryside of southwest France. He has an eclectic style ranging from realism to fantasy with a particular interest in wildlife painting, producing highly detailed, enchanting images with a universal appeal. He recently returned to live in the UK, where he continues his passion for watercolor painting. Visit his website to see more: RayShuell.co.uk.

Interior and Cover Designer: Richard Tapp
Art Producer: Sue Bischofberger
Editor: Erum Khan
Production Editor: Andrew Yackira
Illustrations © Ray Shuell, 2020
Author photo courtesy of Logan Schmidt

ISBN: Print 978-1-64739-755-5 | eBook 978-1-64739-456-1

R0

CPSIA information can be obtained
at www.ICGtesting.com
Printed in the USA
JSHW041958210122
22154JS00003B/6